Jazz Songs of Innocence

Bob Chilcott

for SSA, piano, and optional bass and drum kit

Contents

MUSIC DEPARTMENT

Composer's note

Jazz Songs of Innocence is the second jazz-influenced work that I have written for the Crescent City Choral Festival in New Orleans, and I am grateful to Cheryl Dupont, the conductor of the New Orleans Children's Chorus, and all the choirs at the Festival in 2011 for bringing the piece to life.

In these settings the piano part can be played exactly as written, or, equally, the pianist can improvise freely around the given lines. I would encourage the addition of bass and drums, and indeed of any other instruments that would work within the stylistic parameters of the piece.

The poems used in this collection are taken from *Songs of Innocence* by William Blake, and date from around 1788–9. They reflect not only thoughts unaffected by the burden of worldliness, but also timeless themes of wisdom and humanity.

Duration: *c.*16 minutes

OXFORD
UNIVERSITY PRESS

Great Clarendon Street, Oxford OX2 6DP, England

First published 2012

ISBN 978-0-19-338156-8

Music and text origination by Enigma Music Production Services, Amersham, Bucks
Printed in Great Britain on acid-free paper by Halstan & Co. Ltd, Amersham, Bucks

to Cheryl Dupont and the New Orleans Children's Chorus
for the Crescent City Choral Festival, 2011, with thanks for
ten years of joyful collaboration

Jazz Songs of Innocence

1. Piping down the valleys wild

William Blake (1757–1827)

BOB CHILCOTT

*The piano part can be played as written or used as a guide. Bass and drum kit can join *ad lib.*

Printed in Great Britain

9
cloud I saw a child, And he laugh - ing said to me: 'Pipe a
cloud I saw a child, And he laugh - ing said to me: 'Pipe a

13
unis.
song a - bout a lamb.' So I piped with mer - ry cheer, 'Pi - per,
song a - bout a lamb.' So I piped with mer - ry cheer, 'Pi - per,

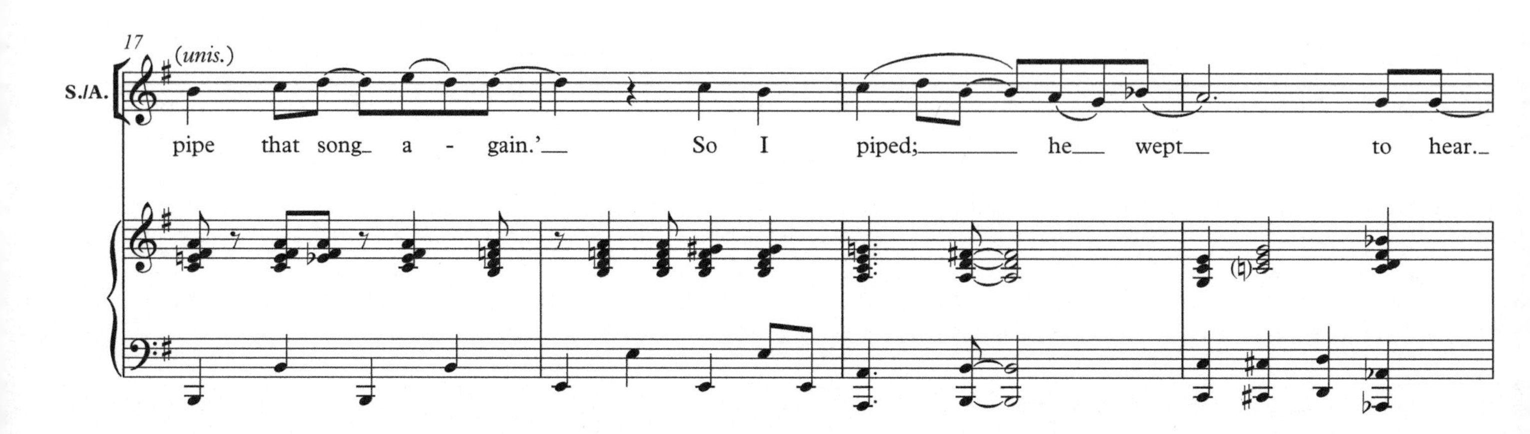
17
(unis.)
S./A.
pipe that song a - gain.' So I piped; he wept to hear.

21

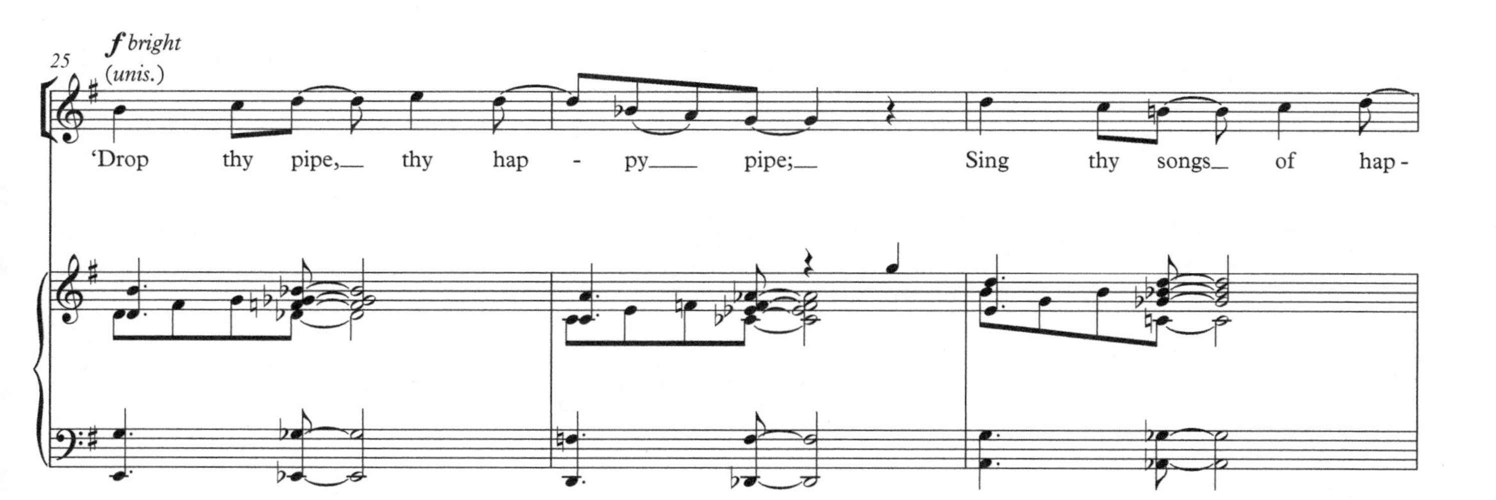
f bright
25
(unis.)
'Drop thy pipe,__ thy hap - py__ pipe;__ Sing thy songs__ of hap -

28
- py cheer.' So I sung the same__ a - gain, While he wept with joy__ to__ hear.__

32
S. 1
S. 2
'Pi - per, sit thee down and write In a book that all may read—'
A.
'Pi - per, sit thee down and write In a book that all may read—'

36
unis.
So he van - ished from my sight. And I plucked a hol - low reed,
So he van - ished from my sight. And I plucked a hol - low reed,

40
ff
And I made a rur - al pen, And I stained the wa - ter clear,
ff
And I made a rur - al pen, And I stained the wa - ter clear,
ff

44
unis.
And I wrote my hap - py songs Ev - 'ry child may joy
And I wrote my hap - py songs Ev - 'ry child may joy

48
to hear, ev - 'ry child may joy
to hear, ev - 'ry child may joy

52
to hear, ev - 'ry child may joy to hear.
to hear, ev - 'ry child may joy to hear.

2. The Lamb

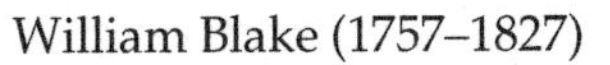

BOB CHILCOTT

mp
Soft - est cloth - ing wool - ly bright;
Gave thee such a ten - der voice,
mp
Mak-ing all the vales re - joice,
mak - ing all the vales re - joice:
Lit-tle Lamb, who made thee?
Dost thou know who made thee?
p
p

*To avoid dividing the alto section, the upper alto line may be sung by the second sopranos.

mf ma dolce
I a child and thou a lamb,
We are called by his name,
we are called by his name.
mp
child
oo
mf ma dolce
we are called by his name,
mf ma dolce
Lit-tle Lamb, God bless thee,
Lit-tle Lamb, God bless thee.
unis.
his name.
Lit-tle Lamb, God bless thee,
Lit-tle Lamb, God bless thee.
rit.
oo
God bless thee.
oo
God bless thee.
rit.

3. The Little Boy Lost/The Little Boy Found

William Blake (1757–1827)

BOB CHILCOTT

13
mf
Speak, fa - ther, speak to your lit - tle boy, Or else I shall be
mf

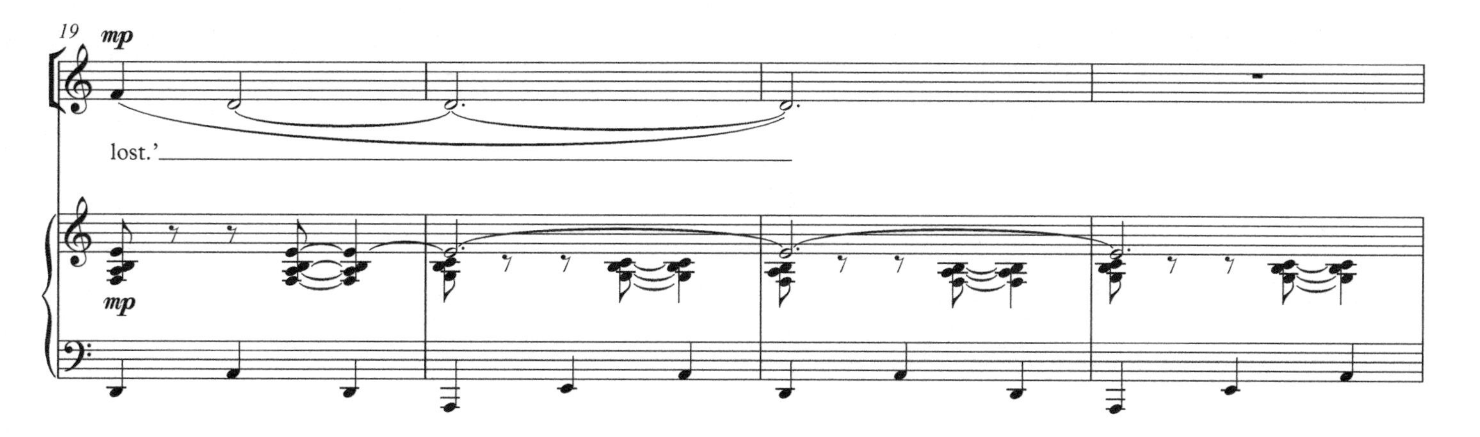
19
mp
lost.'
mp

23

27
S. 1
S. 2
mp
'Fa - ther, fa - ther, where are you
A.
mp
'Fa - ther, fa - ther, where are you go - ing?

31
go - ing? Oh do not walk so fast.
Oh do not walk so fast.
35
mf
ah
Or else I shall be
mf
Speak, fa - ther, speak to your lit - tle boy, Or else I shall be
mf

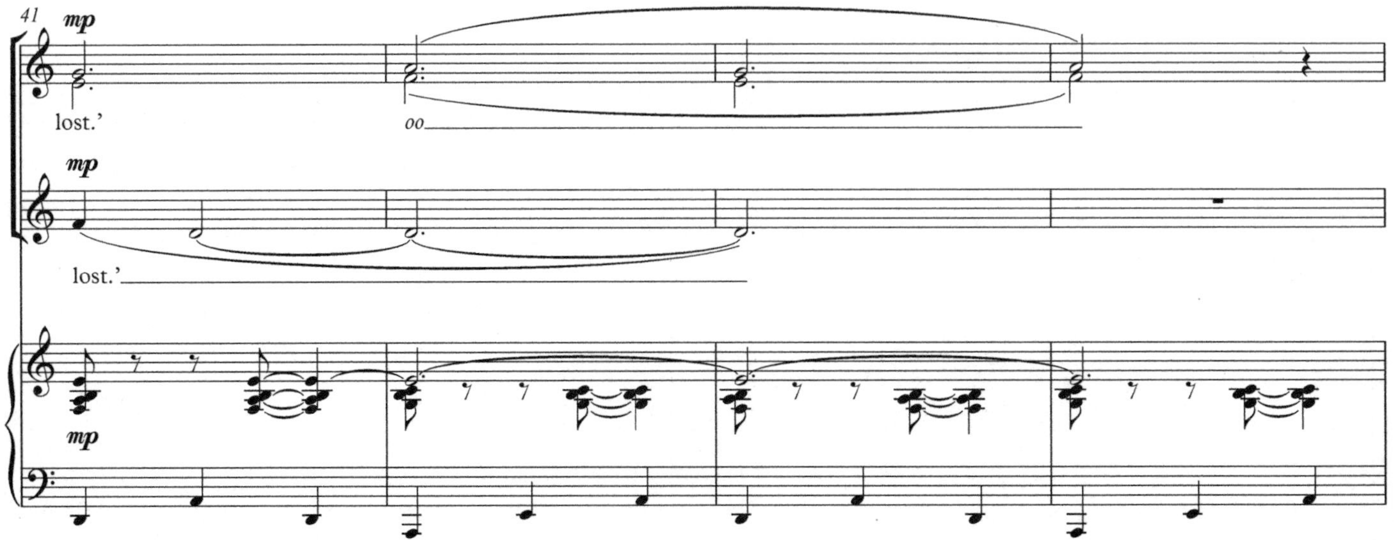
41
mp
lost.'
oo
mp
lost.'
mp

45
mp
oo
The
mp
The
49
unis.
S./A.
mf
S.
A.
night was dark, no fa - ther was there, The child was
mf
54
unis.
mp
wet with dew. The mire was deep, and the
mp
59
mf
S.
A.
unis.
child did weep, And a - way the va - pour flew.
mf

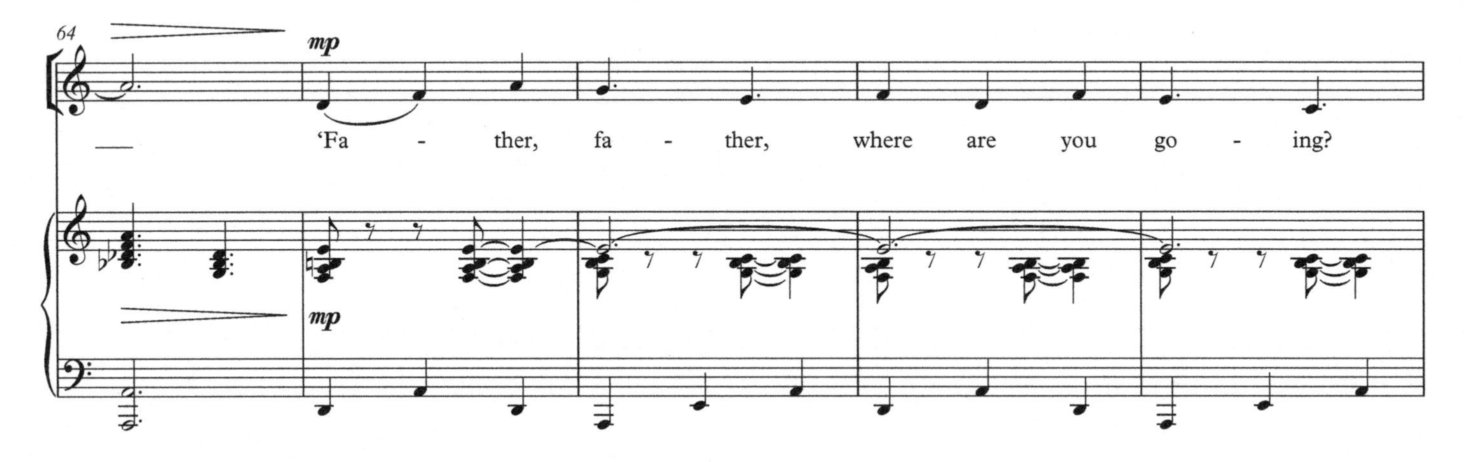
64
mp
'Fa - ther, fa - ther, where are you go - ing?
mp

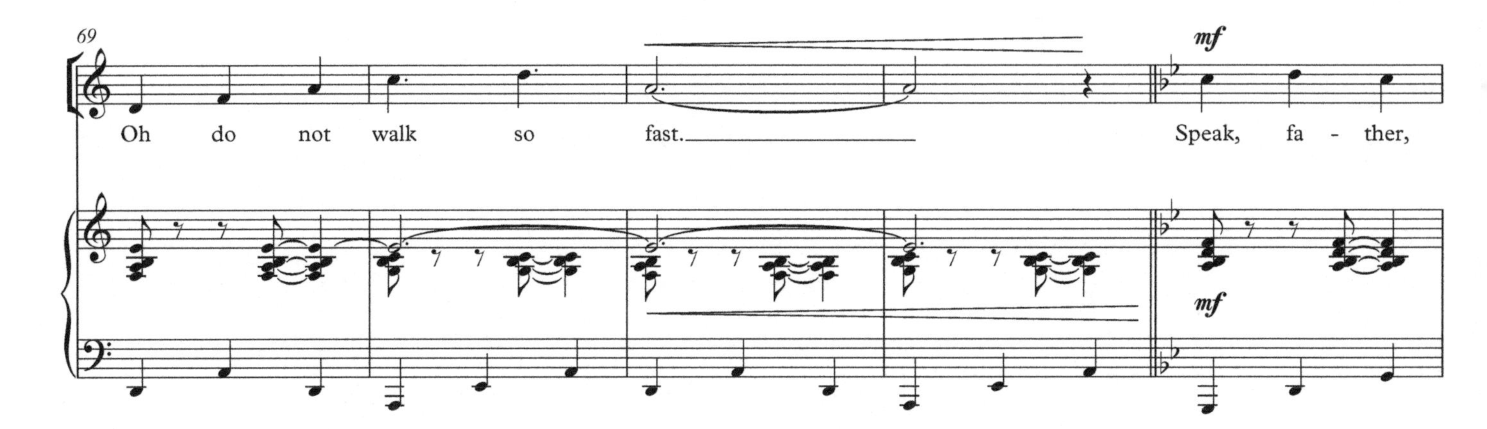
69
mf
Oh do not walk so fast. Speak, fa - ther,
mf

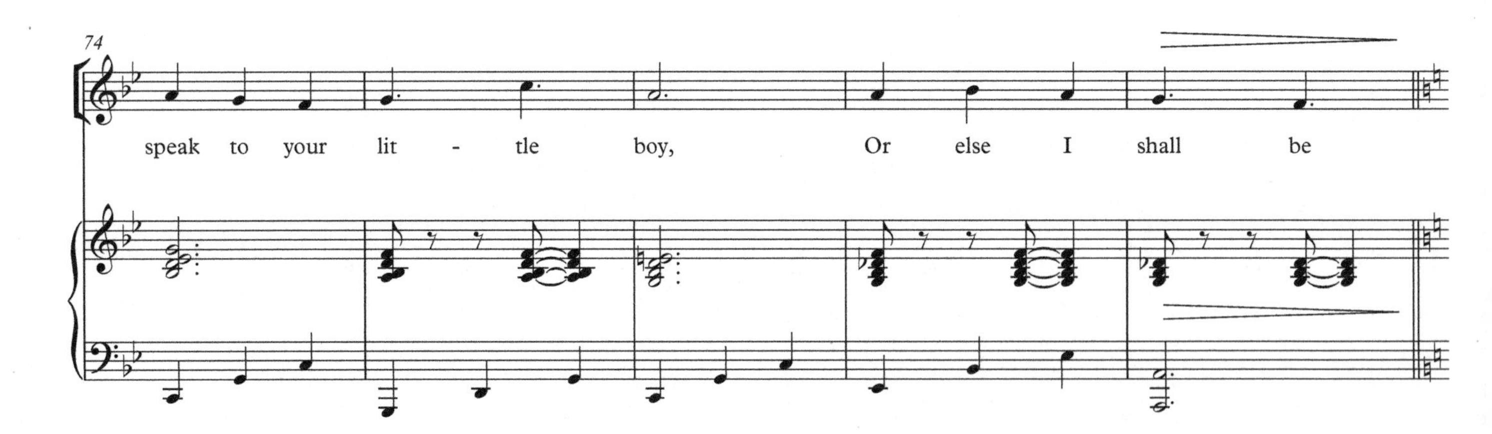
74
speak to your lit - tle boy, Or else I shall be

79
mp
lost.'
mp

83
87
unis. mp
. 1/2
Fa - ther, fa - ther,
A.
mp
Fa - ther, fa - ther,
91
Fa - ther, fa - ther,
Fa - ther, fa - ther,

95
unis. p dim.
Fa - ther, fa - ther.
p dim.
unis.
Fa - ther, fa - ther.
p dim.
pp
100
Expressive ♩ = c.56
A.
p sost.
104 ALTOS p dolce espress.
The lit-tle boy lost in the lone - ly fen,
Led by the wand'r - ing light,
mp espress.
Be-gan
108
to cry, but God ev - er nigh
Ap-peared like his fa-ther in white.
p
mp espress.
p sost.

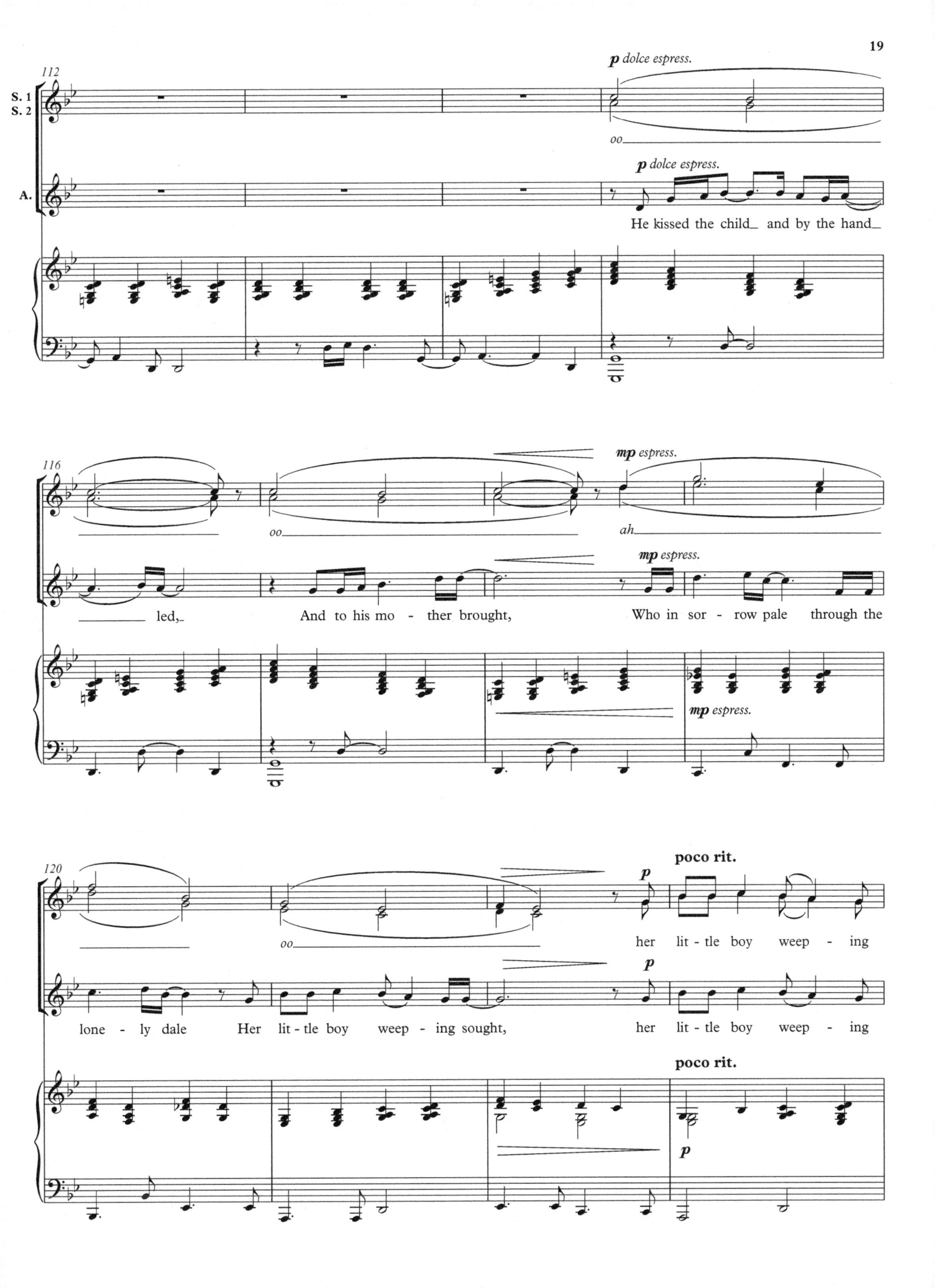
112
S. 1
S. 2
A.
p dolce espress.
oo
p dolce espress.
He kissed the child_ and by the hand_
116
mp espress.
oo
ah
mp espress.
led,_
And to his mo - ther brought,
Who in sor - row pale through the
mp espress.
120
poco rit.
p
oo
her lit - tle boy weep - ing
p
lone - ly dale Her lit - tle boy weep - ing sought,
her lit - tle boy weep - ing
poco rit.
p

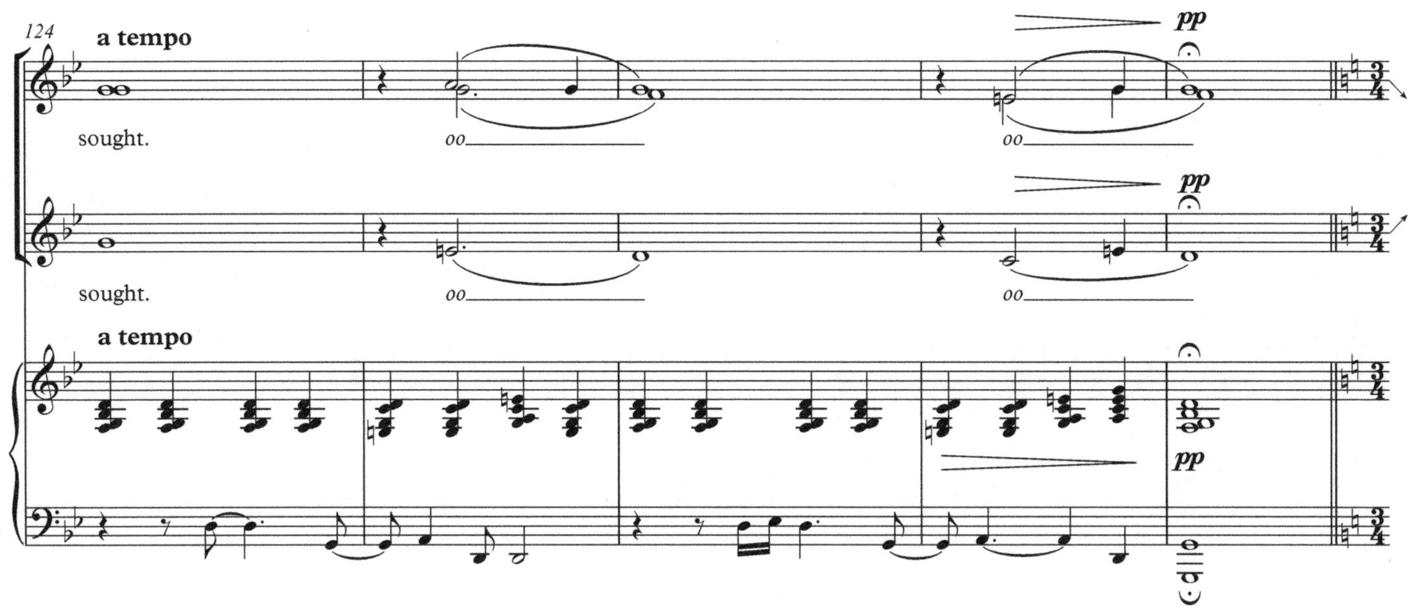
124
a tempo
pp
sought.
oo
oo
pp
sought.
oo
oo
a tempo
pp

129
Tempo I
S./A.
mp

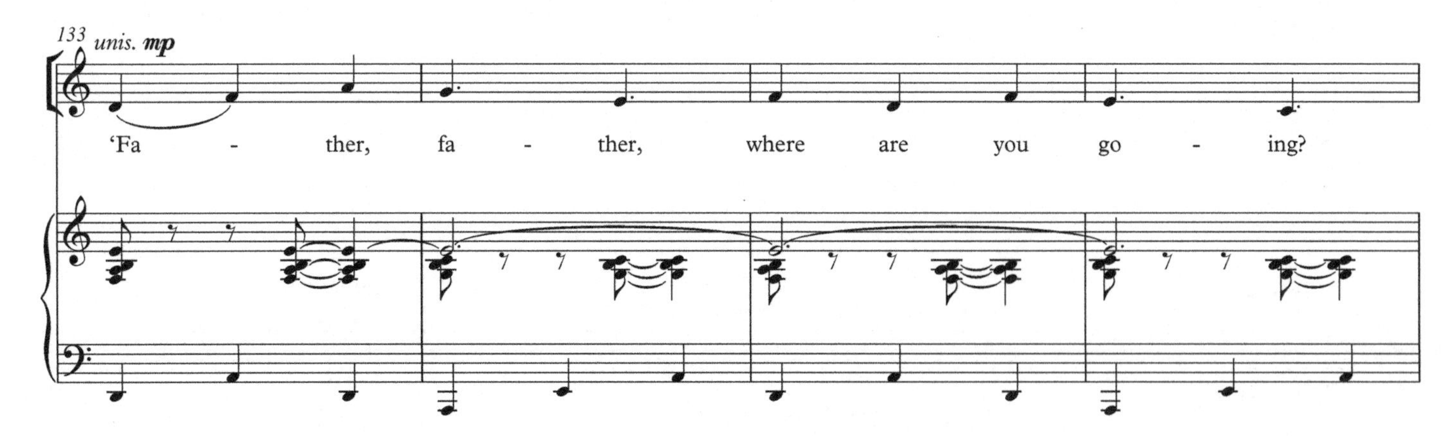
133
unis. mp
'Fa - ther, fa - ther, where are you go - ing?

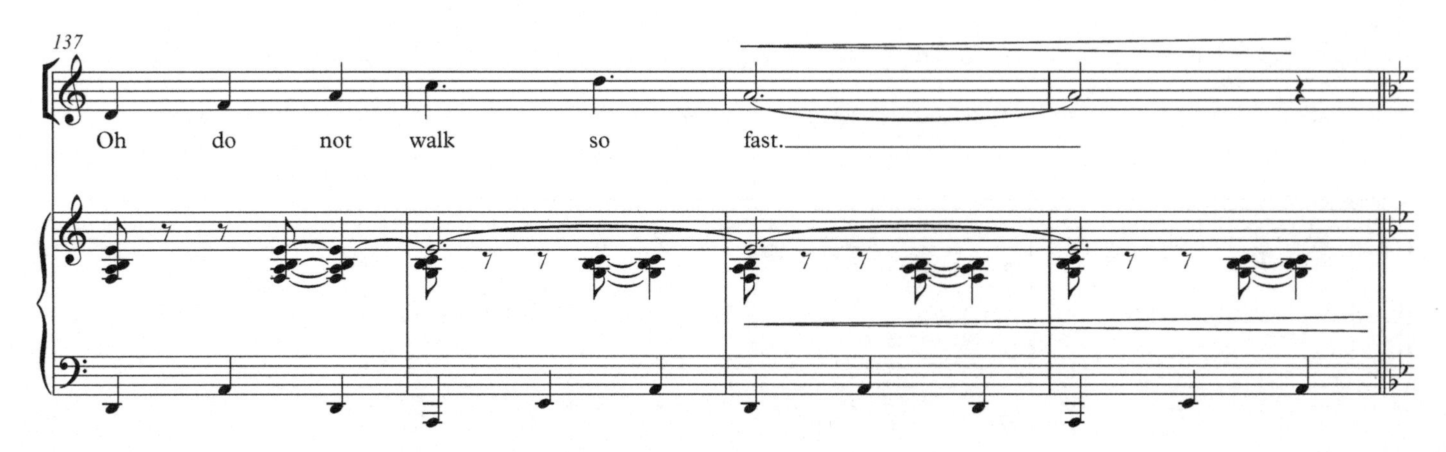
137
Oh do not walk so fast.

141
mf
Speak, fa - ther, speak to your lit - tle boy, Or else I shall be
mf

147
mp
lost.'
mp

151

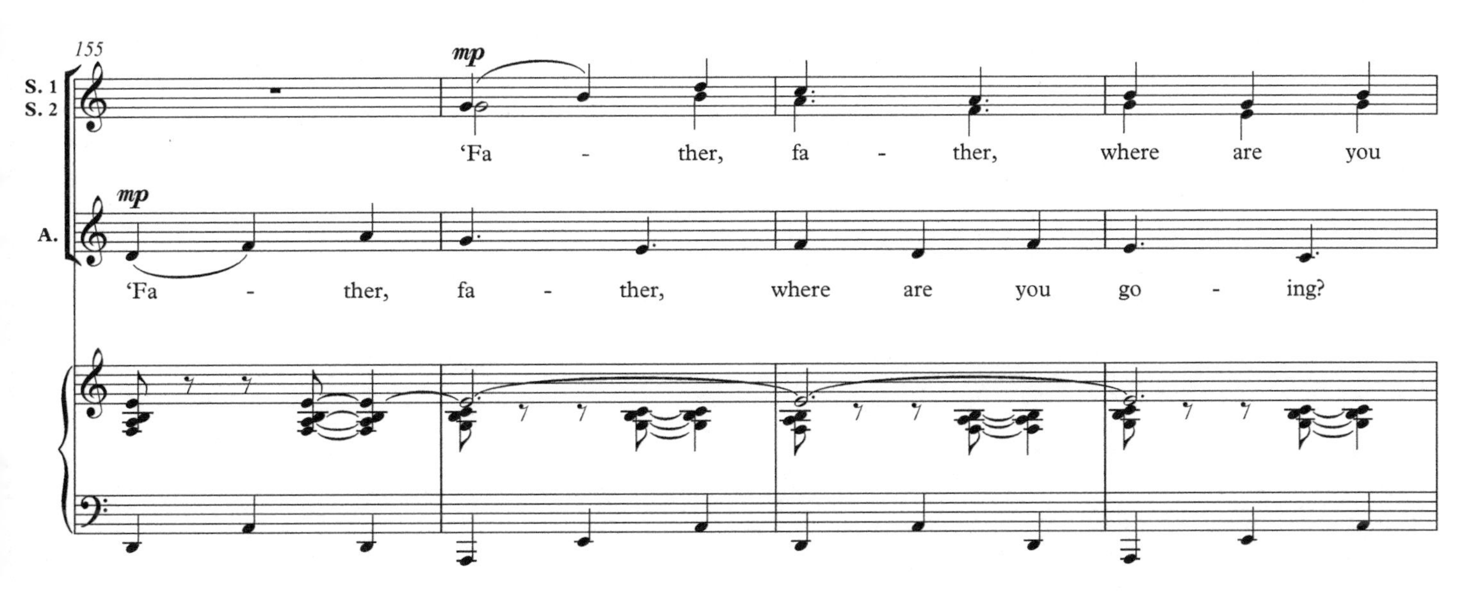
155
S. 1
S. 2
mp
'Fa - ther, fa - ther, where are you
mp
A.
'Fa - ther, fa - ther, where are you go - ing?

159
go - ing? Oh do not walk so fast.
Oh do not walk so fast.
163
mf
ah
Or else I shall be
mf
Speak, fa - ther, speak to your lit - tle boy,
Or else I shall be
mf
169
mp
lost.'
oo
mp
lost.'
mp

173
oo
mp
Fa - ther,
178
fa - ther,
Fa - ther, fa - ther,
mp
Fa - ther, fa - ther,
Fa - ther,
184
unis. p dim.
Fa - ther, fa - ther.
p dim.
unis.
fa - ther,
Fa - ther, fa - ther.
p dim.
pp
8vb

4. The Echoing Green

13
S. 1
S. 2
A.
sports shall be seen On the e - cho-ing green, While our sports shall be seen On the
youth time were seen On the e - cho-ing green, In our youth time were seen On the
sports shall be seen On the e - cho-ing green, While our sports shall be seen On the
youth time were seen On the e - cho-ing green, In our youth time were seen On the

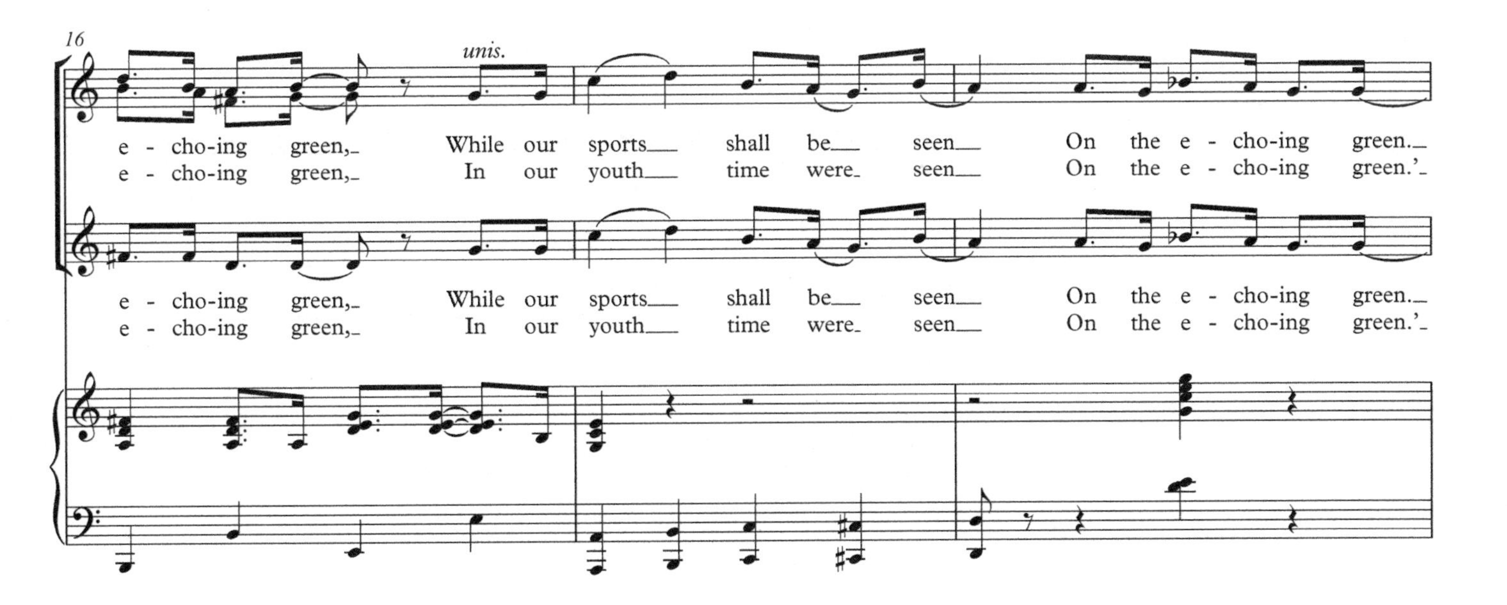
16
unis.
e - cho-ing green, While our sports shall be seen On the e - cho-ing green.
e - cho-ing green, In our youth time were seen On the e - cho-ing green.'
e - cho-ing green, While our sports shall be seen On the e - cho-ing green.
e - cho-ing green, In our youth time were seen On the e - cho-ing green.'

19
1.
f
2.Old
f
2.Old
1.

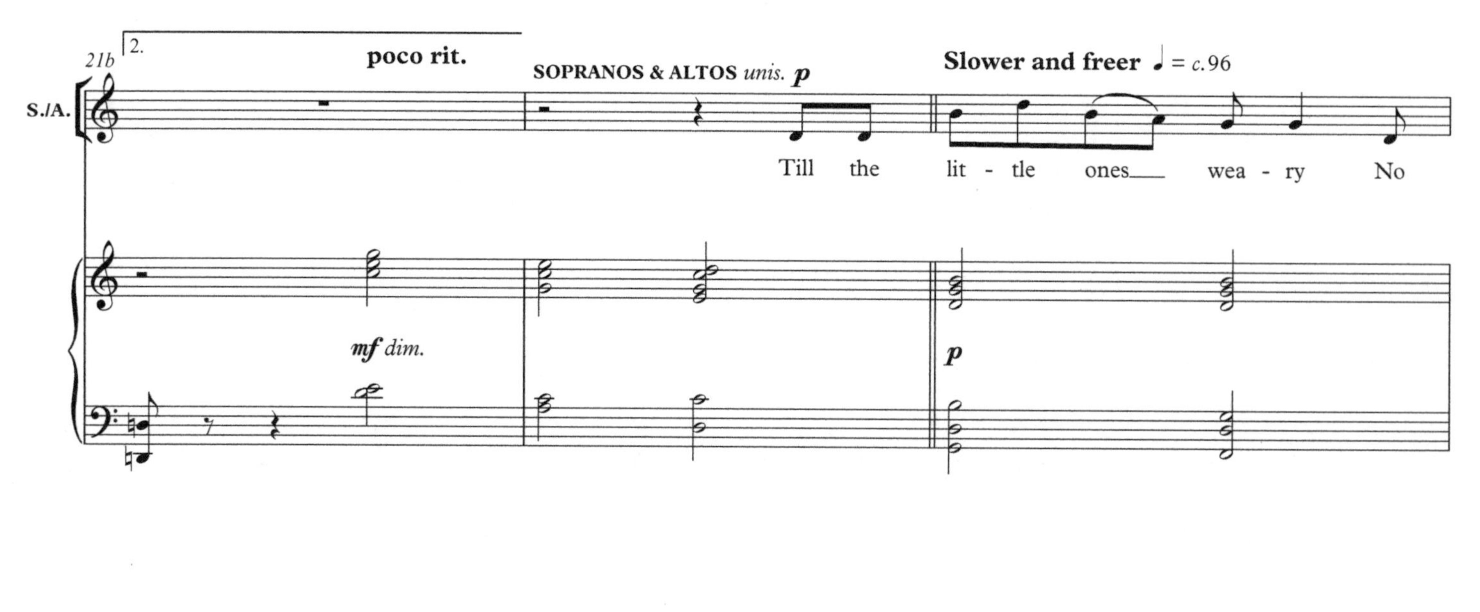
21b
2.
poco rit.
S./A.
SOPRANOS & ALTOS unis. p
Slower and freer ♩ = c.96
Till the lit - tle ones___ wea - ry No
mf dim.
p

24
more___ can be mer - ry; The sun does de - scend, And our sports have an end. Round the

27
laps___ of their mo - thers, Ma - ny sis - ters and___ bro - thers, Like birds in their nest, Are___

30
S. 1
S. 2
mp
rea - dy for rest; And sport no more seen On the dark - en - ing green, And
A.
mp
rea - dy for rest; And sport no more seen On the dark - en - ing green, And
mp
33
unis.
sport no more seen On the dark - en - ing green, And sport no more seen
sport no more seen On the dark - en - ing green, And sport no more seen
36
poco rit.
Tempo I
f
On the dark - en - ing green. The sun does a - rise, And make
f
On the dark - en - ing green. The sun does a - rise, And make
poco rit.
Tempo I
f

39
hap - py the skies.__ The mer - ry bells____ ring To____
hap - py the skies.__ The mer - ry bells____ ring To____
41
unis.
wel - come__ the Spring. The sky - lark and thrush, The
wel - come__ the Spring. The sky - lark and thrush, The
43
birds__ of the bush, Sing loud - er a - round, To the bells' cheer - ful sound, While our
birds__ of the bush, Sing loud - er a - round, To the bells' cheer - ful sound, While our
gliss.

46
sports shall be seen On the e - cho-ing green, While our sports shall be seen On the
sports shall be seen On the e - cho-ing green, While our sports shall be seen On the
49
unis.
e - cho-ing green, While our sports shall be seen On the e - cho-ing green,
ff
e - cho-ing green, While our sports shall be seen On the e - cho-ing green,
ff
52
unis. fff con forza
On the e - cho-ing green.
fff con forza
On the e - cho-ing green.
ff
fff

5. The Divine Image

William Blake (1757–1827)

BOB CHILCOTT

13
mf
- tress, And to these vir - tues of de - light Re -
mf
- tress, And to these vir - tues of de - light Re -
mf
16
p dolce
poco rit.
unis.
- turn their thank - ful - ness, re - turn their thank - ful - ness, their thank - ful -
p dolce
- turn their thank - ful - ness, re - turn their thank - ful - ness, their thank - ful -
poco rit.
p dolce
19 a tempo
poco rit.
- ness.
- ness.
a tempo
poco rit.

a tempo
For Mer-cy, Pi - ty, Peace and Love Is God our fa - ther
For Mer-cy, Pi - ty, Peace and Love Is God our fa - ther
a tempo
dear, And Mer-cy, Pi - ty, Peace and Love Is
dear, And Mer-cy, Pi - ty, Peace and Love Is
p dolce
poco rit.
unis.
Man his child and care, is Man his child and care, Man his child and
Man his child and care, is Man his child and care, Man his child and
poco rit.
p dolce

a tempo
care.
care.
a tempo
mp
mf
For Mer - cy has a hu - man heart, Pi - ty a hu - man face, a
mf
For Mer - cy has a hu - man heart, Pi - ty a hu - man face, a
mf
hu - man face, And Love, the hu - man form di - vine, And Peace, the hu - man
hu - man face, And Love, the hu - man form di - vine, And Peace, the hu - man

42
dress, the hu - man dress.
f
Then ev - 'ry man of
dress, the hu - man dress.
Then ev - 'ry man of
45
ev - 'ry clime That prays in his dis - tress,
ev - 'ry clime That prays in his dis - tress,
48
Prays to the hu - man form di - vine: Love, Mer - cy, Pi - ty, Peace, Love,
mf dim.
unis.
Prays to the hu - man form di - vine: Love, Mer - cy, Pi - ty, Peace, Love,
mf dim.

poco rit.
a tempo
51
Mer - cy, Pi - ty, Peace.
Mer - cy, Pi - ty, Peace.
poco rit.
a tempo
mf dim.
p
3
54
poco rit.
a tempo
p dolcissimo
And all must love the
p dolcissimo
And all must love the
poco rit.
a tempo
mp
p dolcissimo
3
57
3
mp
hu - man form, In hea - then, Turk or Jew.
3
mp
hu - man form, In hea - then, Turk or Jew.
mp

Processed in England by Enigma Music Production Services, Amersham, Bucks.
Printed in England by Halstan & Co. Ltd, Amersham, Bucks.